Poetry

FOR
INSPIRATION, FAITH, TRUTH AND HEALING

Where We Are Now Series.

VOLUME 1

Sharon Cully

WHERE WE ARE NOW

Copyright © 2014 Sharon Cully

The moral right of Sharon Cully to be identified as the Author of the work and Emma Jarvis as the Artist has been asserted by them in accordance with the Copyright, Designs and Patents Act 1988. All rights reserved. No part of this book may be used or reproduced by any means, graphic, electronic, or mechanical, including photocopying, recording, taping or by any information storage retrieval system without the written permission of the publisher except in the case of brief quotations embodied in critical articles and reviews.

National Library of Australia Cataloguing-in-Publication entry
Author: Cully, Sharon, author.
Title: Poetry for Inspiration, Faith, Truth and Healing / Sharon Cully ; Emma Jarvis, artist.
ISBN: 9780992365301 (paperback)
Series: Where We are Now – Past and Future; Volume 1.
Other Authors/Contributors: Jarvis, Emma, artist.

Dewey Number: A821.4
Publishing Details
Published in Australia

Printed & Channel Distribution in US/UK/AUS / Canada
Printed through Lightning Source (USA/UK/AUS)
Available via:

Printed & Channel Distribution in US/UK/Canada/Aus
Lightning Source (USA/UK/AUS)
Available via:
United States - Ingram Book Company; Amazon.com; Baker & Taylor and others
Canada - Chapters Indigo; Amazon Canada and others
United Kingdom - Amazon.com; Bertrams; Book Depository Ltd; Gardners; Mallory International and others
Australia - DA Information Services; The Nile; Emporium Books Online; James Bennet (Australian Libraries) Dennis Jones and Associates; and others

For further exploration any of the material contained within this book the following contact details have been provided:

Written By: Sharon Cully. Where We are Now – Past and Future
Web Site: www.wherewearenow.com.au
Email: sharon@wherewearenow.com.au

Illustrated by: Emma Jarvis. Multidimensional Energy Patterns
Web Site: www.energypatterns.net
Email: mdenergypatterns@gmail.com

Table of Contents

Preface	iv
Acknowledgements	v
In the Depths of Me	1
The Silence Within	3
A Bird's Song	4
Love	6
Change	8
Transformation	11
Faith	13
Dream	16
Surviving on the Journey	19
Grief	22
Pain	25
Hope	28
Loss	31
Fear	33
Sharon Cully - Author	35
Emma Jarvis - Artist	37

PREFACE

My life has been a rich one with a roller-coaster of emotions. I have been a Registered Nurse for thirty nine years. Nursing combined with my personal experiences has helped me form a deep understanding about the journey we are all on. I have been on my knees more times than I care to remember. In the end it was discovering the saving power, grace and love of God that helped me rise. Rise beyond the turmoil and trauma that this life put before me. So I found that quite without meaning to I have been working on an experiential "How to survive" manual. The skills I developed; usually the hard way, have enabled me to provide an ongoing, deep and satisfying service to others from all walks of life.

Along this journey I discovered the gift for expressing these emotions through the written word. These words now come as poetry and hold the key to overcoming. This collection of poems came from the very heart of me. With the love of God, together we have been able to lay them here for others who may find themselves in need of comfort. Each poem has its own unique illustrated pattern providing the reader with maximum benefit along with these words. The patterns depict the words of each poem demonstrated in energy form. These have been provided by my daughter who also shares her gifts given from God for the benefit of others.

ACKNOWLEDGEMENTS

No collection of words is complete without the acknowledgement of those who have supported the process. Thanks must go to my family who have supported and loved me throughout all these times in my life. They always help me climb up the ladder again.

My husband Peter has often been left to cope with finishing of the evening meal as I am apt to disappear for hours as a new idea arrived.

My mother Eileen who passed on her gift of writing and poetry to me.

My father Bert who listened for hours to all my strange musings.

My daughter Emma proof reader extraordinaire. I thank you for the gift of your illustrated multidimensional energy patterns that provide additional comfort on many levels to those who read these poems.

My children Peter and Michael for putting up with my eccentricities and loving me anyway.

For all the people who have coloured my tapestry of life I thank you.

Above all I give my thanks to God, who has been there at every moment to herald my strengths and to supply Grace to my failings.

In the Depths of Me

Deep down in the very depths of me;
I ponder the true meaning of Life.
Like a seed that sprouts and knows;
like a bud that unfurls and grows.

There is a Truth to uncover;
past memories to remember.
New memories that will reveal my true purpose outlaid;
as the reality of this world starts to waver and fade.

A spark, a flame or a glow;
from deep within or below.
That awakens, reminds me to learn and to know;
that which sustains and allows me to grow.

Into a Human that is being;
into a Human that is knowing.
A presence luminous and glowing;
with a purpose that directs my life out-flowing.

Frustration and confusion fade instead;
upholding and comforting others in this present time and ahead.
I seek that close union with God and so know;
which convoluted path is the right one to follow.

I discover the Joy and the Wonder;
of reaching out to all persons near and asunder.
I am an integral part of the greatest story of All;
God, the "I Am", I hear and answer your call.

I sometimes puzzle, reflect and wonder;
why so many humans don't take the time to ponder.
They miss the true purpose of this life with its treasure;
as they strive only for more pleasure and leisure.

On this journey of eternal design;
that exists before and after this time.
I move ever forward on this journey of mine;
this, the true destiny of all Human Kind.

The Silence Within

Somewhere deep inside is a place.
A place, I can hide from the world.
Here I can find silence;
a place that doesn't need a fence.

This place throbs with a silent force.
There is no division, me or them.
Here my tension and fears ebb away;
a place where I love to linger, stay and pray.

I converse and pray to my closest friend.
I converse and pray to the one who knows me best.
Here I can meditate and listen in the silence;
feeling, waiting for my Divine Guidance.

In this place of silence, I feel no pain.
No longer is there any loss or gain.
As if, in a cocoon of love without fear or strife;
I feel this connection to the very fabric of life.

A Bird's Song

A bird's song plays the very fibres of my heart.
The caressing strokes that awaken and start;
the total infusion of my senses with harmony.
That uplifts my Soul with the Cosmic Melody.

I tremble and feel the tremulous sound.
It strives to free itself and new cravings abound;
as it rises and falls in rhythmic waves.
It's very essence provides me with a peace that saves.

My heart rises from its earthly chain.
My mind rejuvenates from melody's falling rain;
my Soul thirsts, remembers, rises and drifts.
My Soul searches the infinite oceans of time and lifts.

My skin awakens trembles and then craves.
My hairs rise as one to reach these rhythmic waves;
of a harmony that soothes and caresses me.
It engulfs me like a welcoming sea.

A bird's song heals pain.
A bird's song awakens and then anchors my belief;
in a higher state of living and being.
Reminding me that I am truly a Human...Being!

LOVE

Love is like a flower.
Coaxed by the sun;
unfolding a little to bare.
Its innermost secrets are revealed to share.

A Being that desires to live.
Risking the strife and the sharp cuts of a knife;
chancing it all for that moment of pleasure.
Two will come together.

Explore and share the portals of eternity.
Those that beckon and whisper;
leading us to experience a true belonging.
We find the fulfilment of our innermost longing.

On the arc of a rainbow and in beams of light.
This love feels so very, very right;
that awakens deep inside us.
Love is All and will always onward lead us.

Love is always worth it.
Love conquers all;
in the face of love, everything else in life begins to pall.
Without it, the human heart would slow and stall.

Change

Change is in the air.
I can smell and feel it.
I can taste, hear and see it.
Change threatens my very existence, as I see it.
I know to survive I must cease to fear it.

I start to shake inside and I know.
I need to let go and just flow.
Like the whim of the tide I must just go.
I reveal my uncertainty.
I will let down the fences of my security.

Those erected to keep me in and others out.
I am not ready, my inner truths to flout.
I tremble and hesitate seeking an easier route.
Still I always return back.
Back to this reality and the strength I lack.

Flow I must, waving like grasses in the sea, to and fro.
This way, that way, go with the flow.
I wonder where I will be tomorrow.
Do I really need to know?
Can I really just simply let go?

Yesterday has passed.
I need to know God and hold fast.
Tomorrow may never come.
Try not to look back.
The past often shows where I have gone off track.

Let go of fear.
The time is finally here.
Instead watch eagerly.
Move with the tide.
Never look back or hide.

Watch everything unfold with anticipation.
Like the dawn of a new creation.
See but don't react.
Continue on this Higher Power to trust.
To hold on tight to God now is a must.

Instead walk the tight-rope.
Find deep within that comfort and hope.
Find the Truth, Faith and Integrity.
Move forward, just one step at a time.
Breathe, just one breath at a time.

Listen, hear and feel the Divine.
God continues to sing and woo this heart of mine.
My Soul whispers to me so softly.
Love, forever beckons me on.
I will finish what I have begun.

With my God, the original Source.
That God of Love and the Creation force.
I will finally know my True Self and all Humanity.
I will know the true meaning of Divinity.
I know now that this is but a single moment in eternity.

Transformation

It is time to die.
It is time to fly.
Why then do I continue trying to find a different Way?
When throughout this journey and all along;
I know where and to whom I belong.

To resist is futile.
I must go that extra mile.
Follow that path over the bridge.
Move from one reality over to the next.
Rest, breathe and it will all work out for the best.

I rise above my trials, my confidence growing.
I have found my Wisdom and my Inner Knowing.
I know my true home is in Eternity.
I now see the wonders of your Way.
I follow the path and will not stop to stray.

I bow my head in acknowledgement and gratitude for where I have been.
This life is but a prelude to the bigger picture I have seen.
I walk in Faith but never alone.
This Way follows the Light.
I will never waver or lose the sight.

Like moths to a flame.
I stake my claim.
Follow the Truth and the Light.
The veil drops that divides us, as I walk beyond the mire.
Then I feel joy as I find my heart and soul's desire.

The fullness of God's Glory.
My role in the greatest story.
In life I learnt to rise and never give up.
I see the beauty and wonder of all Mankind.
I love this communion and sharing of All, as the Truth I find.

Faith

By faith we know and grow.
We listen and hear;
knowing our belief is still true.
That our path will guide us through.

The truth will be revealed.
The truth has its own way, its own plan;
though others may taunt and mock.
Turned at times into a laughing stock.

We continue on.
One step at a time;
past and future combine.
Into an intricate tapestry divine.

The threads of this tapestry pass us by.
Dancing, turning and teasing;
as they go to who knows where.
Once there, the design created shines rare.

They flutter as they brush pass.
They settle and then anchor each other;
until together they create the design.
The design that grows and spans all time.

This design cares not for our Human time frames.
It runs free and wild with endless possibilities;
while we are left guessing and pondering.
The path's strange wandering.

These threads wander by their own whim.
They respond to circumstance;
not for us to know.
The changing details forever continue to grow.

Reach out and understand this.
Understand and have a say;
but remember freewill is free.
God's touch will guide you and me.

Onward we travel.
The truth behind us begins to unravel;
we should not despair.
This time as we know it, is neither here nor there.

All will be revealed.
When it is meant to be;
without disrespect to you or to me.
Accept this plan and try not to flee.

We continue to journey on.
We gather pace;
accept this journey is mystery.
Mystery of our destiny.

Such is the scope of God's creation.
With our time-frame in eternity;
life's journey will continue to unfurl and grow.
Life is showing us the way to a new tomorrow.

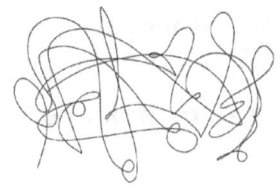

Dream

Close your eyes and dream.
Travel away on a light beam.
Away from this life;
with its pleasures and strife.

Close your eyes and go to bed.
Stay quiet and still, as if dead.
Except for the slightest of eyelid flutter;
as your day's events your mind reruns, over and over like a stutter.

Then with sleep there is a freedom to rise.
Freedom to ponder and surmise.
The shackles and restraints dropping;
off the body you live in.

You drift and you float.
Like an airship or boat.
Aboard the cosmic train;
taking you far from life's fast lane.

The past and the future become one.
Just as deep down you knew they always had done.
You can be great or you can be small;
humble or tall.

You can truly fly.
You have only to really believe and try.
Move away and beyond this place;
visit different realms in infinite space.

The joy to feel such freedom.
Is like welcoming God's Kingdom.
Compared to living in this place;
with its separation between people and its non-stop pace.

In a dream you can be young or old.
You can be alone, or your lover in your arms enfold.
In your dreams you can sail away on a sea;
floating, drifting and totally free.

You wait all day for this blessed escape.
Far away from the confines of this landscape.
Your soul yearns to stretch and be free;
to move away from this prison, this body that is thee.

Your dreams nurture your soul.
Your dreams heal you and make you whole.
Inspiration and guidance will find you there;
with comfort, friendship and love to share.

All your needs will be met.
You will never again forget.
There is this oasis that you can nightly escape to;
whilst this complicated life pathway you clamber through.

Oh dream to smell the roses.
Feel no need for pretence and poses.
Instead, be free in this moment;
this feeling is heaven sent.

So settle to sleep each and every night.
Think only of things joyous and bright;
then you will dream and be free;
to come ride the cosmic light beams with me.

Surviving on the Journey

The way ahead seems blocked.
Legs feel shackled and locked.
Mud seems to cling and hold down your feet.
You seem to have to push through tempest and sleet.

You rise above for one moment in time.
Then you bottom out again and recommence the climb.
That one moment though, felt heaven sent.
One whiff and taste reminds you of what Jesus meant.

There is a way.
Come what may.
We can do it.
The lamp has been lit.

You only need to remember and turn.
Face the light and see its bright burn.
So bright.
So light.

Like moths to the flame.
There is no-one to blame.
You can get it wrong.
You can take too long.

To see the way shown by Jesus.
To remember he walks so near us.
One moment at a time.
One breath at a time.

That is all we need to do.
God's Grace will see you through.
Think and do what you know is right.
Watch closely and follow the light.

The door is ajar.
I can see the light from afar.
Onward and upward, never look back.
Everything behind you is shrouded in black.

Overcoming and victory will be thine.
You just continue to climb and to climb.
The door is ajar.
The light is now nearer than far.

There you can see God's Face.
There you can feel God's Grace.
You will feel at home in this place.
Far away from the rat-race.

You will feel God's Grace and Love.
Staying with you, as you felt it above.
You need to stay true to God's Purpose.
It will help you survive in our life's circus.

The Way is right.
It leads you to the Light.
There you will experience the power and the might.
It will allow your heart to take flight.

As you walk this life path with God's Grace.
You can apply grace to Life's intricate lace.
The way becomes clear.
Love and Healing are always near.

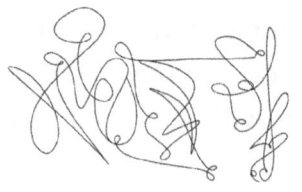

GRIEF

Dead stop, I feel hit by a train.
No breath, there is only pain;
only a void and the icy cold.
A chasm with its iron-grip hold.

Life ceases to be.
The world seems to disappear before me;
frozen in limbo with no movement.
Just me and the surrounding firmament.

I am suspended in time.
I am unable to find;
a foot hold or a niche.
I grasp as I fall into the abyss.

There is a thick and tangible silence.
It keeps out the threatened violence;
wrapping me up tight in a cocoon.
I feel smothered, breathless and swoon.

The scream choked down, finally arrives.
Then it breaks out and strives;
coming from deep down struggling to be free.
It finally wrenches itself out of me.

A deep ache replaces the pain.
This ache seeps through every part of me like soaking rain;
hanging on and sticking like glue.
It will remain with me now whatever I go through.

Very slowly, the pulse of life returns.
I moan and I groan as my heart yearns;
wanting a different day, a happier place.
Finally I come to realise, that this reality is what I must face.

I hear a whisper and then a murmur.
Insects recommence their life song with fervour;
flying again, the birds begin to sing.
The world restarts its background harmonising.

The world has begun to return.
My heart prefers the world to spurn;
no, no, no and no!
I don't want it to be so.

But the world and life stays.
It reaches out and plays;
coaching me on.
Eventually, it teaches me let go and move on.

This difficult life path I know has its reason.
At times though, it can feel like an act of treason;
grieving steals the will to live from me.
All I wanted was to be happy and free.

Slowly, softly life pads by.
Time passes on and I begin to try;
one minute at a time.
Then one day at a time.

The sun peeps over the clouds again.
The laughter of children, a singing wren;
coming back for my attention.
Forcing me to remember, this world full of life and sensation.

My wound is finally soothed.
My pain and sorrow seem to have finally moved;
far away for a time.
I now move on, live and continue this journey of mine.

Pain

Pain is a wakeup call.
It reminds me to listen to me and the All.
My body is crying.
Parts of me are suffering and even dying.

Listen can you hear?
Can you feel the tremble and the fear?
Something does not feel right.
It overcomes me taking over like blight.

Pain is a warning.
Pain is a yearning.
From deep down inside I need to understand.
What it is preventing me from being able to withhold and stand.

I hold my breath.
I try to breathe again afresh.
Pain still grabs me tight.
I try to resist with all might.

Pain feels like a shackle and chain.
I struggle to overcome in vain.
I want release from pain's grip.
I weaken and slip.

I stand beaten.
I face my fear and dread.
I know I must find a way.
I must work with this pain in my life and let it stay.

Pain may stay a short time.
Or pain may stay for all time.
I must learn to accept this way.
I listen and walk onward come what may.

Pain is like a volcano that has risen.
Pain's purpose is to make me stop and listen.
It helps me search, locate and find.
Look for the hidden damage and hurt in my mind.

Find it I must.
Use my inner guidance, inspiration and then trust.
I have this inner knowing.
I need to search and find what its showing.

First I need to listen and find.
There is a small, quiet voice deep in my mind.
Then search out that small discomfort and its reason.
It really isn't my body shouting out treason.

My body is begging me.
I need to lose the fear and to really see.
Pain's job is to remind me and stay near.
God helps me and lets me conquer the fear.

In order to truly live.
I must first learn to forgive.
First myself and then others.
This releases the pain that imprisons me and smothers.

When I choose to keep this pain.
Then peace and contentment is something I can only fain.
True healing comes from the act of forgiveness.
Therein lays the truth about real human greatness.

HOPE

Hope allows me to conceive;
the notion that I dare to believe.
That no matter how bad things may seem;
I can overcome and enter life's true stream.

Far removed from this struggle and strife;
away from the difficulties of this life.
Instead a new perception is born;
where I no longer need, over this issue to mourn.

See this play from the stage of life;
with its pleasure, pain, suffering and strife.
Then I see the beginning of a better way;
I suddenly notice how the grass does lay.

Up sprightly, reaching for the sky;
when trodden on it does not question why.
The blades of grass lean, strive and unfurl again;
reaching up, up to the heavens, reaching for life again.

They bend down and up, down and up;
all blades of grass simply never give up.
Creation of which I am part,
shows God's Way, right from the start.

Feast on the sun;
and on the waters that run.
Bask in the glory;
the wonder of God's Creation Story.

I overcome and continue to believe;
in the true meaning of life to receive.
I continue to love, despite the knocks;
even as my lifeboat rocks.

I see with renewed vision the big picture;
not only this one now, in miniature.
I see beyond life as just one day at a time;
beyond this journey as just one step at a time.

My life is not just to revolve around this;
difficulty is simply a passing moment on my way to bliss.
Jesus taught us there are reasons for living;
there are reasons for giving.

I stop, listen and take time to see;
how the birds still flutter passed me.
I feel the wind, still ruffling my hair;
the sun shining on me and warming me there.

I smell the roses and taste the nectar;
standing straight and upholding God's Sceptre.
At times life around me spins like a whirlpool;
not obeying any Human rule.

When in the whirlpool of life;
finally I'm flung free from strife.
I feel a joy and see;
wonder at this gift of life and our true destiny.

Loss

I have lost something.
I know something is missing.
I sense more than see life passing.

I am functioning every day.
I am walking through life's tasks.
I hide my hollowness behind a variety of masks.

I am never without it.
It accompanies me every day.
It is always there in the shadows along the way.

It is like losing something important.
It is a part of your own self.
It just seems to have gone somewhere in stealth.

I function in autopilot.
I feel a deep numbness somewhere inside.
Deep, deep down it finds a place to hide.

Somehow, to move on, I must find this place.
Recognise its pain and need of Love's balm.
This will soothe, heal and induce inner calm.

Love's balm heals the inner wound.
This wound then provides a receptive, healing bed.
A bed that allows Life's spark to birth again instead.

Nurture this life spark and feed it new life a bit at a time.
Feed it with Faith, Hope and the Love of the Divine.
Slowly, slowly a gentle healing is mine.

Fear

My skin starts to crawl.
The warning sign before the start of my fall.
The tingle starts down at the base of my spine.
It slowly rolls upward in a straight, dead line.

The heart feels squeezed by icy fingers.
Numbness spreads and then lingers.
This, all-consuming, spreading feeling of dread.
It serves to remind me that I am still far from dead.

Roots seem to grow down from my feet.
They anchor me where my body and earth meet.
My heart pounds against my chest wall.
It sounds like resounding canon fire in an empty hall.

Stuck rooted in time.
Listening, feeling the sensations begin to climb.
These sensations force the run and flee command.
They begin to slowly engulf me where I now stand.

Fear is paralysing.
Fear is also galvanising.
It can lock my feet down fast.
Or it can throw me atop a wave rushing past.

Fear can be real or an illusion.
Strive to look and find the reason.
Is this overwhelming reaction justified?
Or is it something I can overcome and push aside?

Three big, slow breaths in and out.
Make this breath go around the body by the long route.
My heart flutters and my body it will wait.
Then my mind clearer now, will discern my fate.

Sharon Cully – Author

Since 1974 I have worked in the Health Care Industry as a Registered Nurse and then in Government and Non-Government Health Service Management. I was also employed to manage systems (Accreditation and Risk Management) in the Public Sector. I have been an Aged Care Assessor, Aged Care Facility Manager, Teacher and Workplace Assessor. This has provided me with extensive experience in the management of people through all types of life traumas and crises. My experience ranged across many cultures and all age groups. My life has been one of service to others and continues to be. On a personal level I have lived through many of the same crises that affect those I care for. I have lived through death, grief, bereavement experiences and chronic illness. These experiences have added additional levels of understanding, empathy and insight into the needs of others. Most importantly, combined it has provided me the best training ground to assist others who now experience these issues themselves. As a child I emigrated from England to Australia with my parents. This taught me about isolation. The difficulties faced by others when removed from their social and family support systems. The traumatic death of my first husband at a very young age caused me to experience an "Out of Body Experience" (OBE) and many other metaphysical/paranormal events. My second husband taught me a different journey associated with self-understanding, self-worth, social roles, social stigma and the inner strength humans are capable of finding in adversity. The most important lesson learnt is that there is no such word as "can't". An escape to the country from an urban upbringing saw the development of skills related to survival on the land, farming and self-sufficiency. It also taught the true meaning of severe physical and financial hardship. I have travelled extensively to different areas of our world. I have lived and worked in urban, rural and remote areas. This has taught me to wonder and love our world with all its diversity of environments and people. Difficult and far reaching personal and professional experiences caused me to search and question the meaning of Life. I reached and searched for God. I searched for the reasons why "bad things happen to good people". I read profusely and the material includes books on philosophy, theology, psychology, astrology, archaeology, quantum healing, reflexology, bio energy fields, healing crystals, and all manner of alternative therapies. (This is only to name a few). My library is extensive.Some of the services I now provide but am not restricted to are:

Life and Spiritual Journey Coaching. Reiki and spiritual healing. Utilizing music, art and colour for healing purposes. I also hold spiritual self-development group meetings and carry out public speaking at reflective workshops. I love life but especially I love writing, art, nature and music.

EMMA JARVIS - ARTIST

There have been many experiences I have encountered and endured in my short life. At times it feels as if I have lived many in this one lifetime. I have had the joy of many unexplained health symptoms and discomfort to accompany my days; and this is not how I would have described it once. I experienced the type of ill health that resulted in the complete devolvement from a strong and independent woman to a frail one not only of physical but of mind and emotion; so destroyed that total dependence on another was essential. The type of ill health that saw me curled up crying to GOD for help that the pain and discomfort could no longer be endured.

Feeling disappointed and abandoned by the medical world I went searching for answers elsewhere. I found spirituality, I found more questions and I found myself. This search went on for some 5 years. I was led on a journey of true self discovery and healing of so many facets; and it was on one of the many paths that this journey directed me to a meditation class in the March of 2011. During a meditation my hand began to tremble and shake and this was the beginning of something very new for me. It was also the beginning of my climb back to health and a new way to help myself, Mother Earth and one day others. Information was coming through my hand in the form of Multidimensional Energy Patterns. It is these patterns which accompany and support the wonderful healing words contained within this book. I hope they bring you as much comfort and strength as I have personally received from them.

www.ingramcontent.com/pod-product-compliance
Lightning Source LLC
Chambersburg PA
CBHW062244300426
44110CB00034B/1922